My Paper Folding Book
Easy Origami
4

Basics of Paper Folding

Follow the instructions carefully before you start paper folding.

Valley Fold
Take a square paper and fold it from the middle. Then, turn the folded paper as shown.

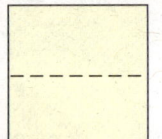

Mountain Fold
Take a square paper and fold it in the middle. Now turn it in such a manner that the folded part is on the top as in the picture.

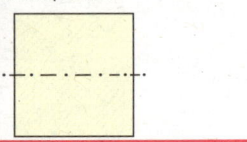

Fold in Front
Take a paper and fold it in the direction of the arrow.

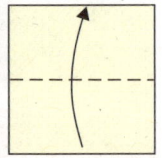

Fold Backwards
Take a paper and fold it backwards as shown.

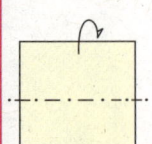

Fold Over and Over
Take a square paper and fold it in a roll as shown.

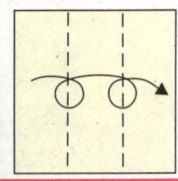

Cut
Use a pair of scissors to make cuts neatly.

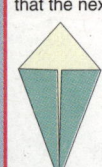 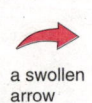 

Enlarge
Whenever a thick arrow is used as an indicator, it means that the next diagram is an enlarged one.

a swollen arrow

Turn Over
Make a paper figure and turn it over as shown.

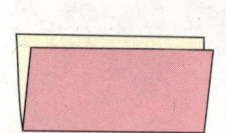

Turn Upside Down
Make a paper figure and turn it upside down as shown.

Making a Crease
Fold and unfold the paper in the required direction gently to get the desired fold. This is a crease.

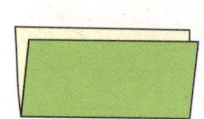

Crease
A faint line which is the result of folding and then opening the fold.

Creased

Stairstep Fold
As the name indicates, this fold is made by combining a Valley Fold and a Mountain to form a kind of pleat or stair step...

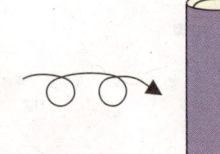

Symmetrical Crease (1)
For a shapely crease, use your thumb-nail as shown in the diagram.

Symmetrical Crease (2)
For a shapely crease, use your nail as shown in the diagram.

Pocket Fold

① Fold the paper into the shape shown. Then fold into half from right to left.

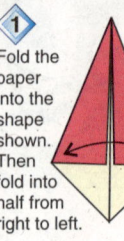

② Now fold the top corner forwards and backwards to make a crease.

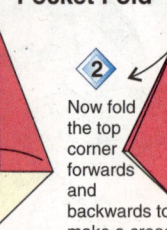

③ Then unfold as the crease is formed.

④ Fold the same top corner again.

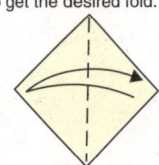

⑤ Fold it to bring it down between the two layers as shown reversing its middle crease.

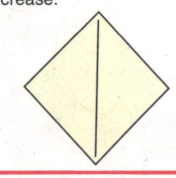

⑥ Your pocket fold is ready.

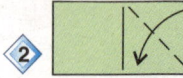

Squash Fold

① Make a mountain fold first. Fold into half and then unfold.

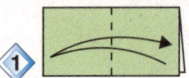

② Fold the top right corner forwards and backwards to make a crease and then unfold.

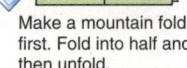

③ Press the top right corner from its upper edge.

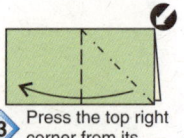

④ Open out the corner into a flattened triangle.

⑤ Your squash fold is ready.

Hood Fold

① Make the shape shown first and then fold into half from left to right.

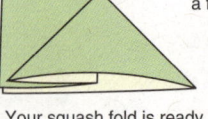

② Fold the top corner forwards and backwards to make a crease.

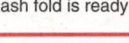

③ When you fold the top, it will look like this.

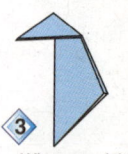

④ Now fold the top corner at the crease inside out...

⑤ .... and reverse its middle.

⑥ Your hood fold is ready.

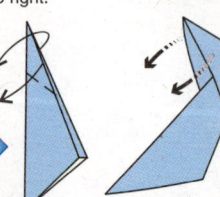 

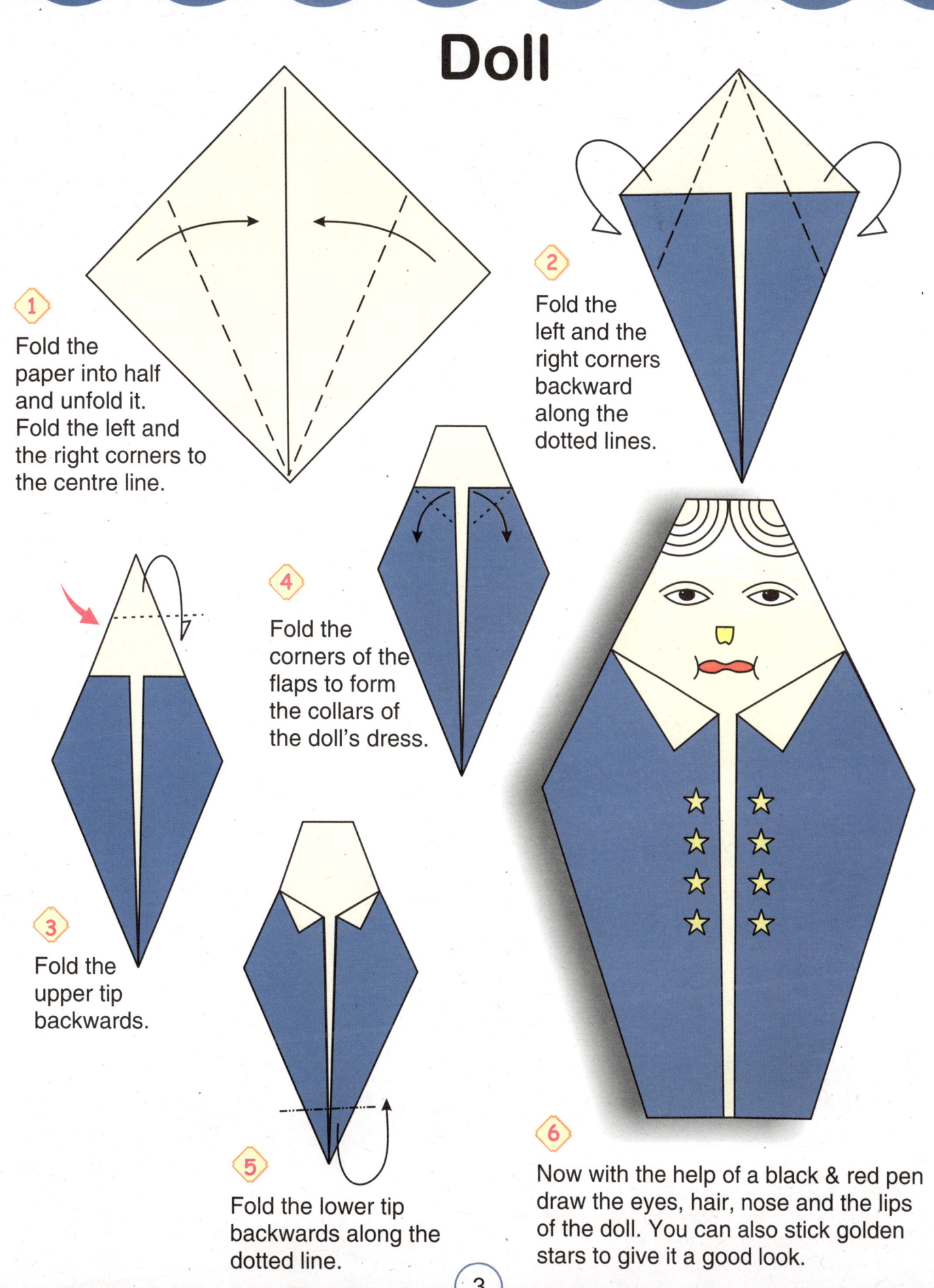

Basket

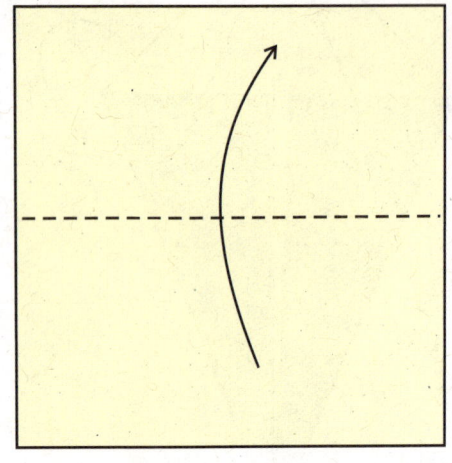

① Fold the paper into half along the dotted line.

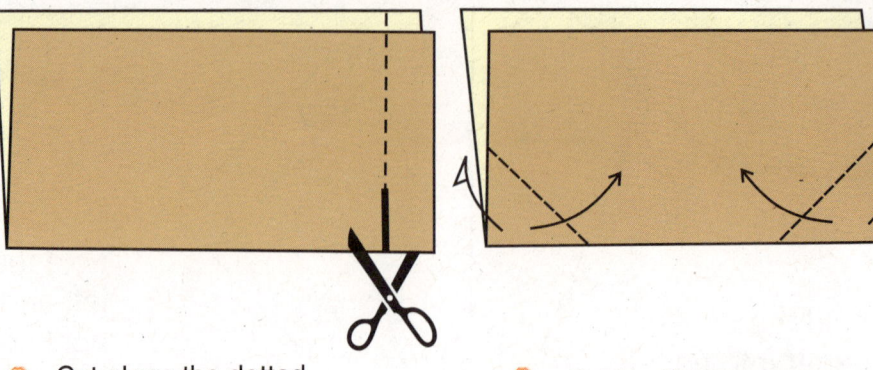

② Cut along the dotted line, half inch from the right edge.

③ Fold both the corners forwards and backwards.

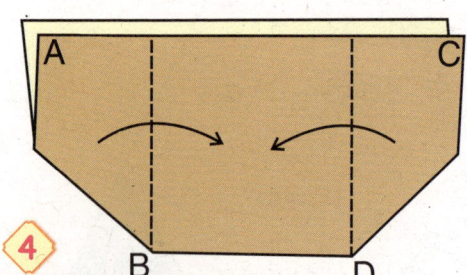

④ Fold AB and CD along the dotted lines to the centre.

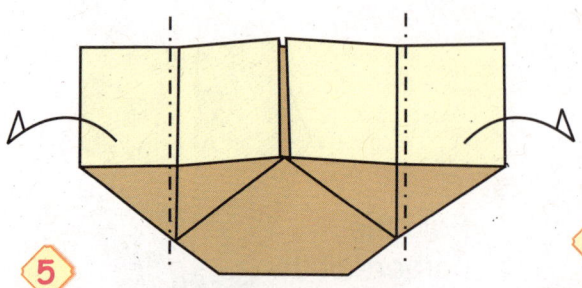

⑤ Fold both the sides of the upper flaps to meet the centre line. Repeat same steps with the back flap.

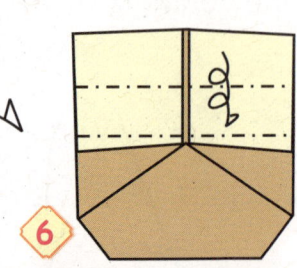

⑥ Fold the front side twice inside, so that the second fold is tucked into the basket.

⑦ Repeat the same step with back flap, so the shape of the basket will be like this.

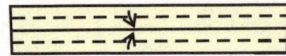

⑧ Now pick the paper strip which you get from the step number 2, and fold in half as shown.

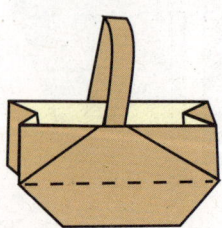

⑨ Paste both ends of the strip to the sides of your basket. Make a sharp crease across the bottom.

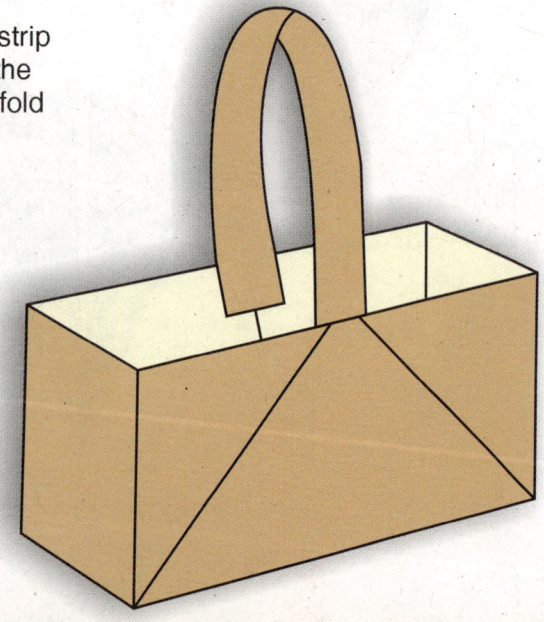

⑩ Open the basket and flatten it at the base. Your holiday basket is ready.

Cow

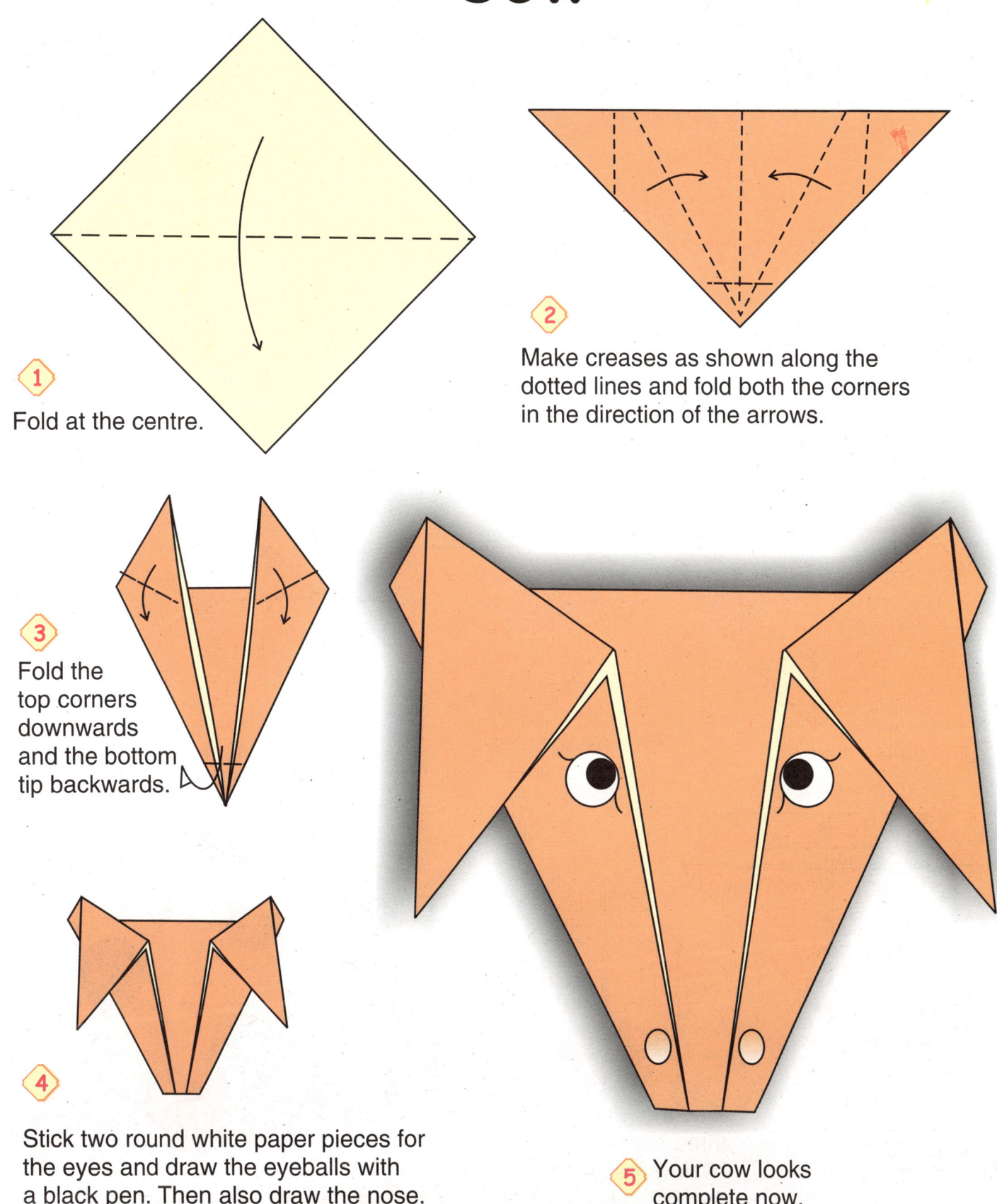

1. Fold at the centre.

2. Make creases as shown along the dotted lines and fold both the corners in the direction of the arrows.

3. Fold the top corners downwards and the bottom tip backwards.

4. Stick two round white paper pieces for the eyes and draw the eyeballs with a black pen. Then also draw the nose.

5. Your cow looks complete now.

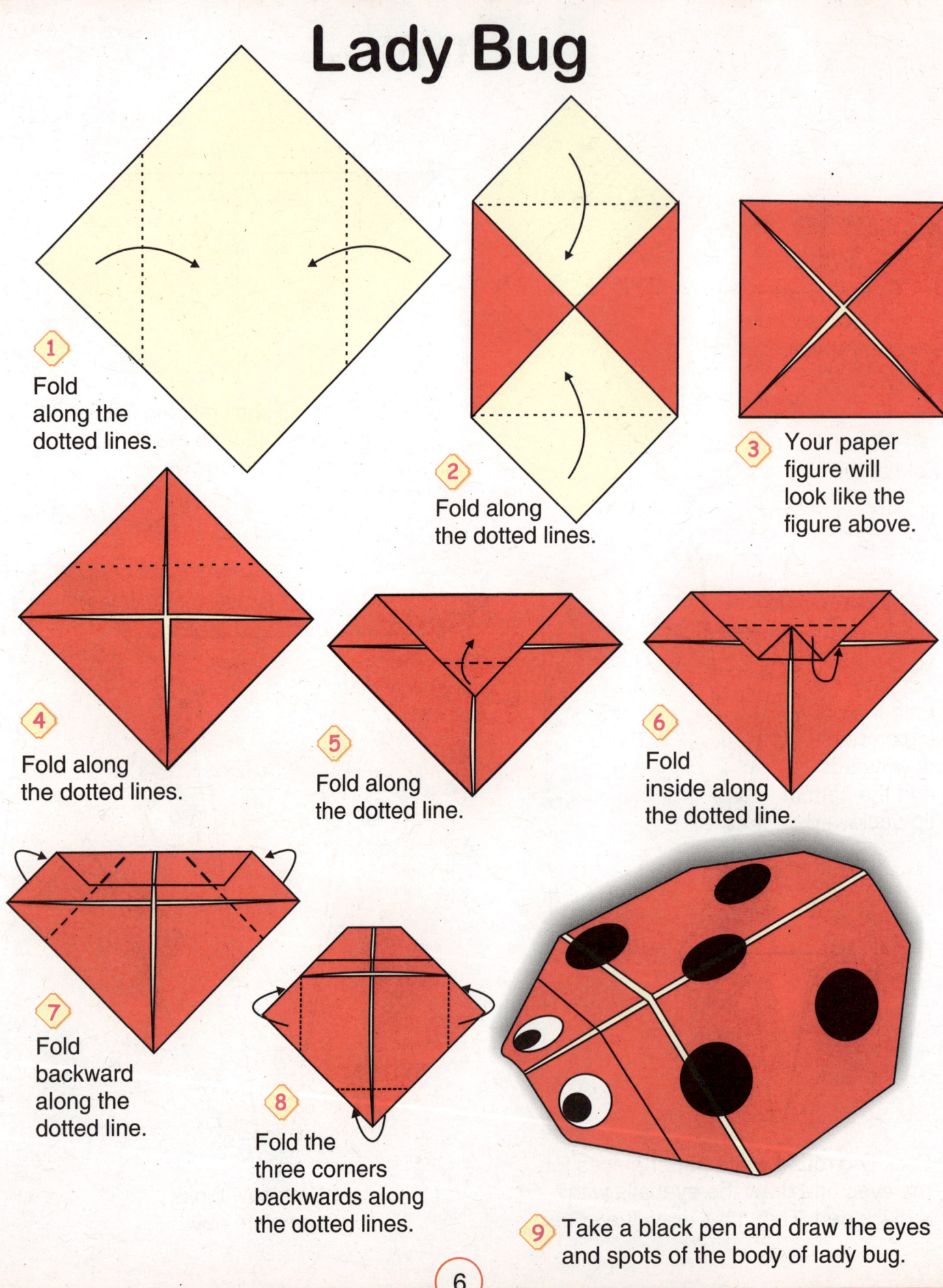

Panda

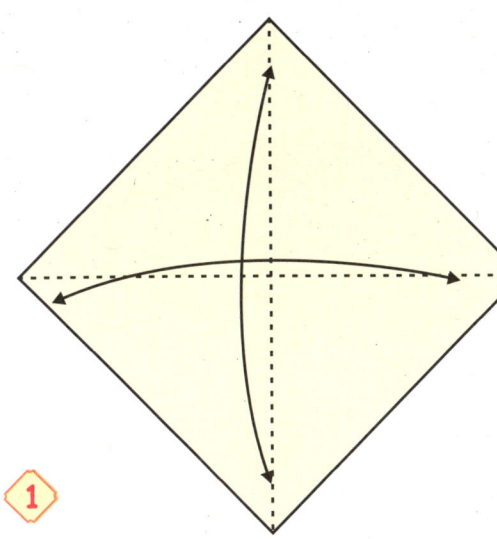

1. Fold a square piece of paper into half at the dotted lines to create creases.

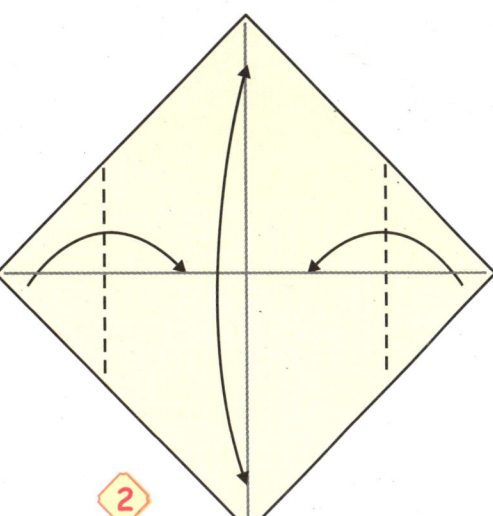

2. Fold the sides along the dotted lines.

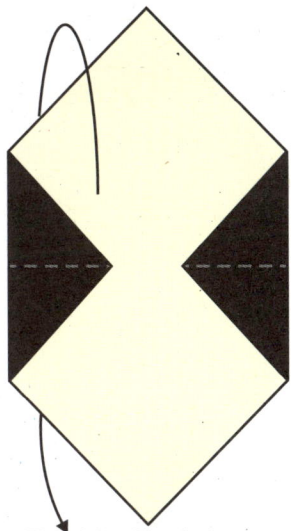

3. Fold half of the paper figure backwards.

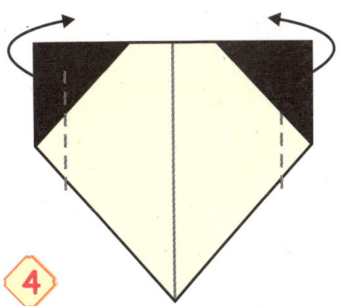

4. Fold the sides backwards along the dotted lines.

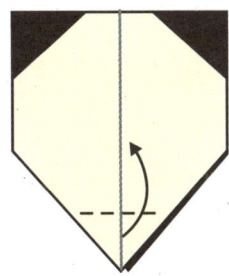

5. Fold the bottom corners upwards along the dotted line.

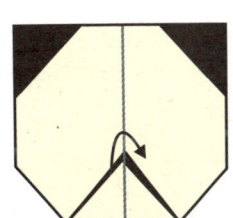 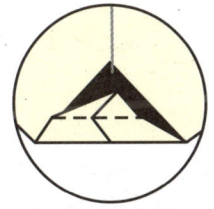

6. Fold the outer layer's tip so that a black triangle is seen.

7. Stick two round papers for the eyes and two white moon-shaped paper pieces for the eyeballs. Your Panda is ready.

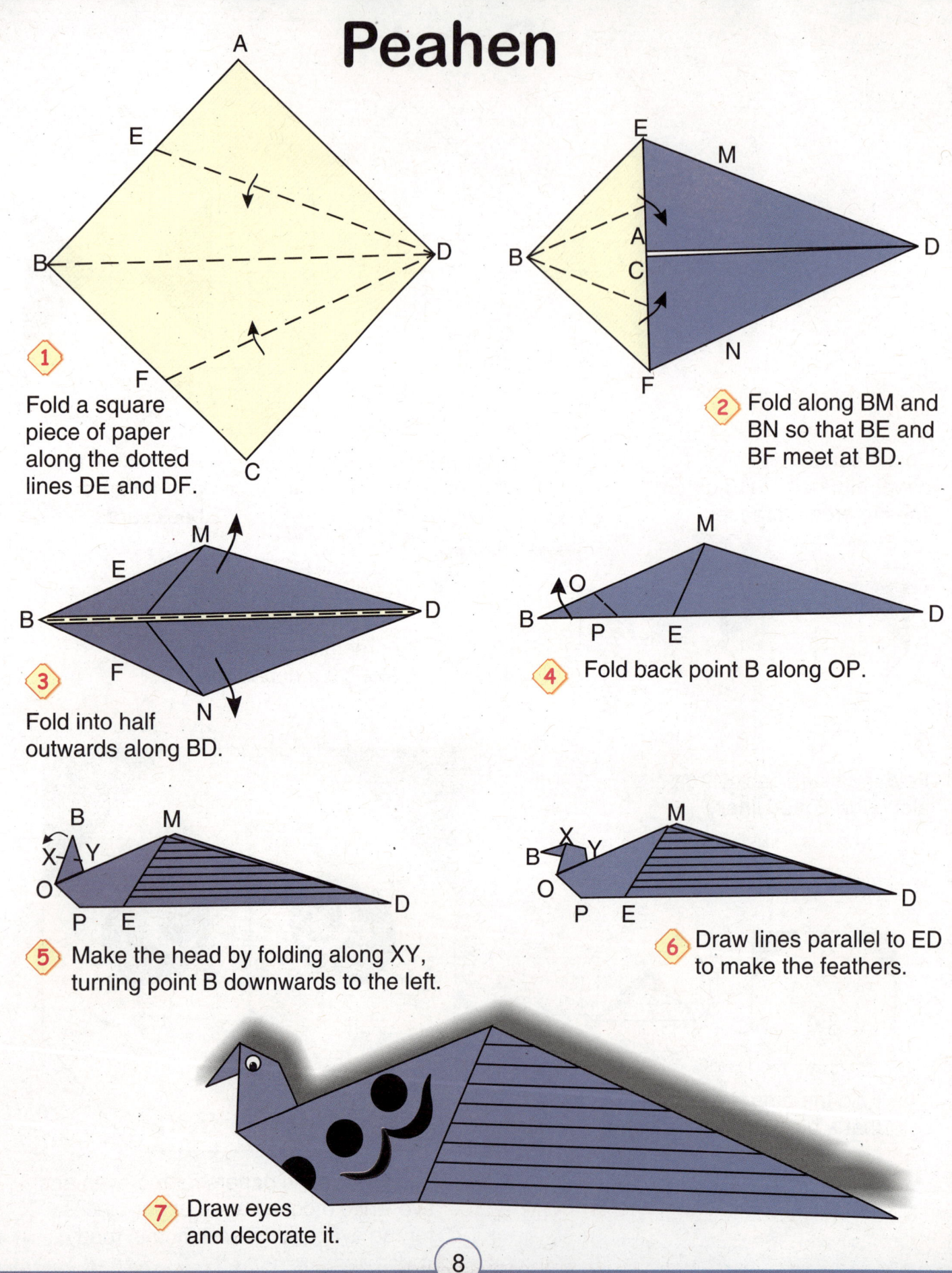

Aeroplane

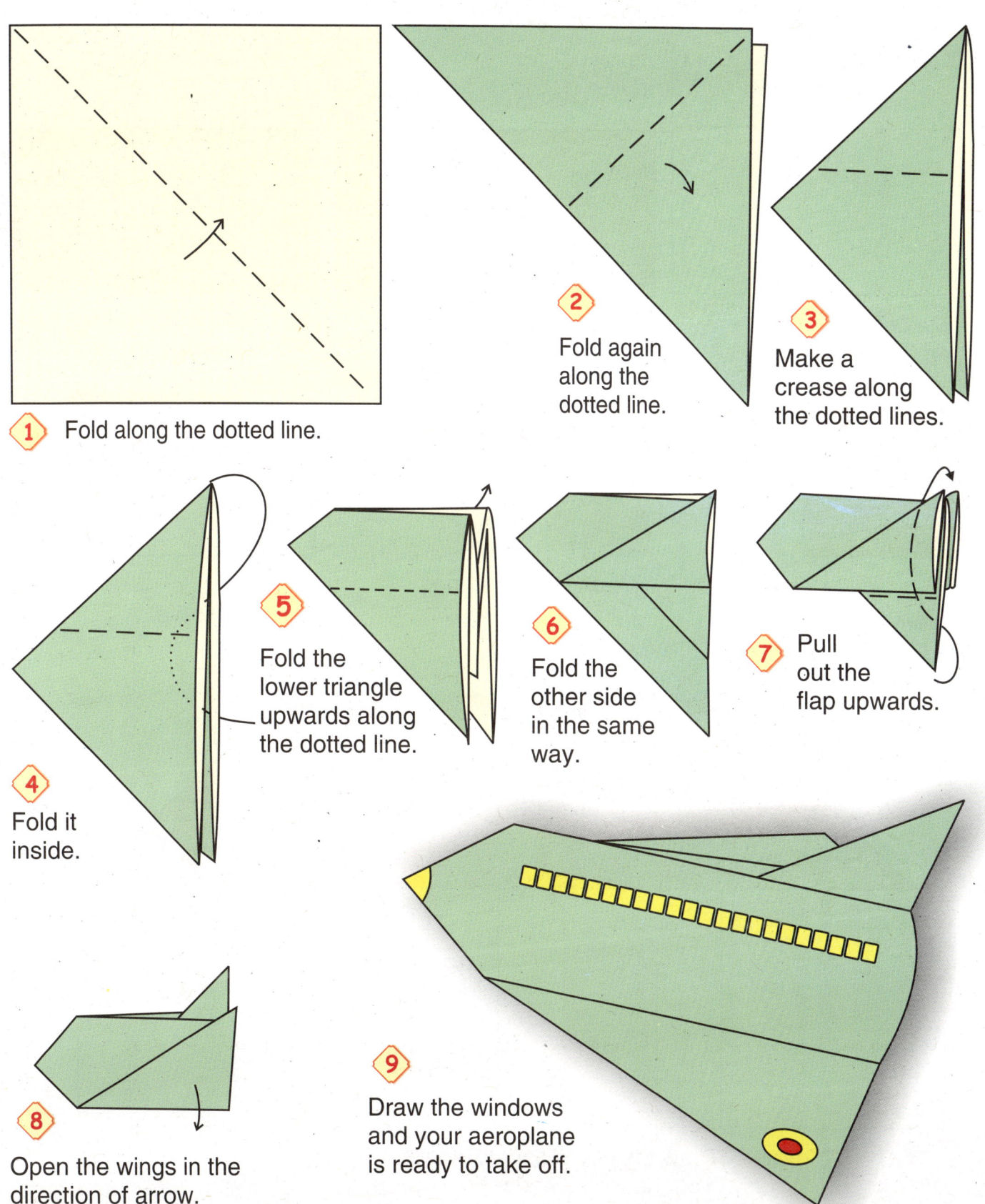

1. Fold along the dotted line.
2. Fold again along the dotted line.
3. Make a crease along the dotted lines.
4. Fold it inside.
5. Fold the lower triangle upwards along the dotted line.
6. Fold the other side in the same way.
7. Pull out the flap upwards.
8. Open the wings in the direction of arrow.
9. Draw the windows and your aeroplane is ready to take off.

House

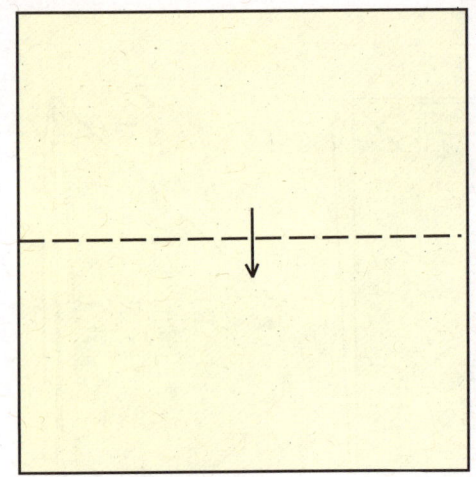

1. Make a centre crease and fold it.

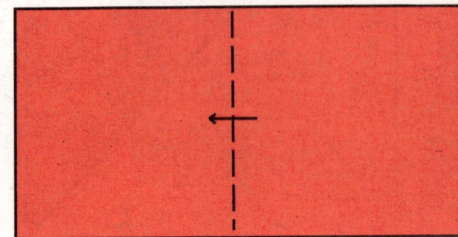

2. Make a crease.

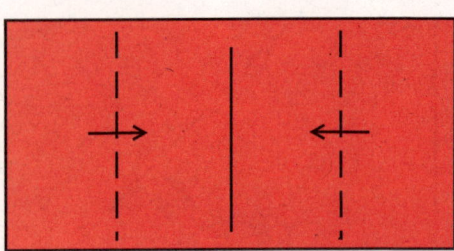

3. Fold both the sides inwards to the centre line.

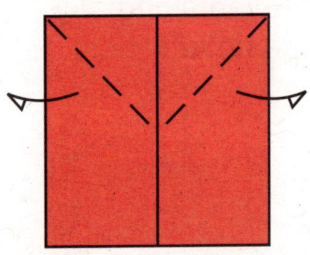

4. Fold from the dotted lines in the direction of arrows.

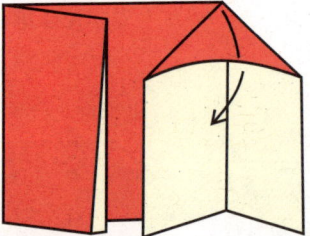

5. Open from the sides and press as shown.

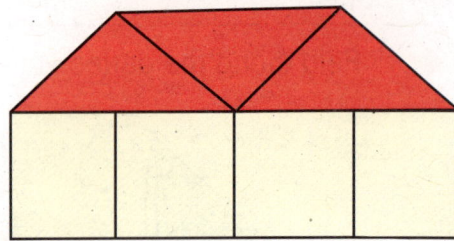

6. Your model will look like the figure above.

7. Draw the doors and windows. Your house is ready.

Pine Tree

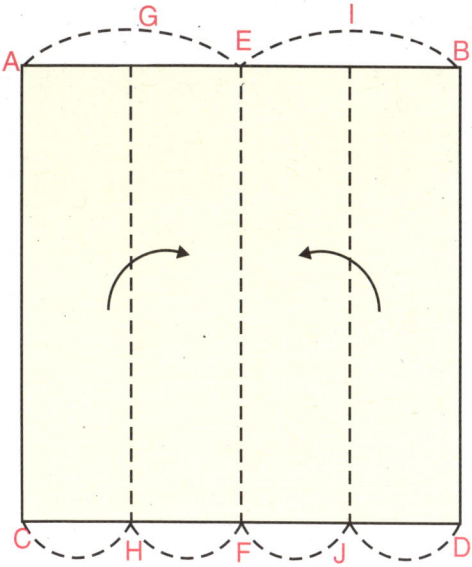

1. Fold along GH and IJ so that edges AC and BD meet at the central line EF.

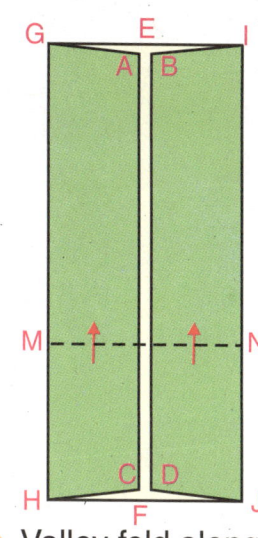

2. Valley fold along MN along the dotted line.

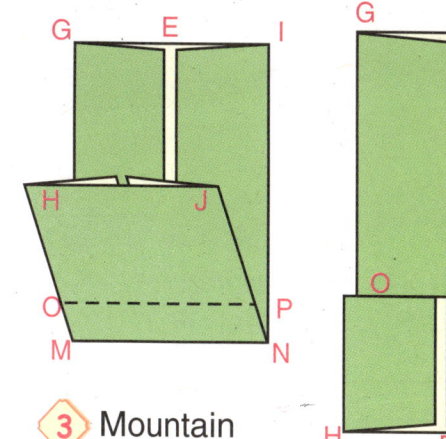

3. Mountain fold along OP.

4. Fold point P so that it overlaps with F.

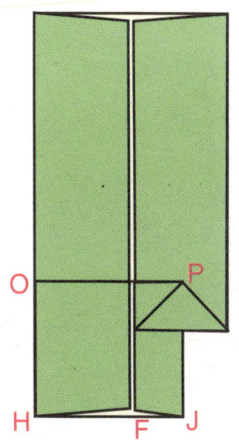

5. Your paper figure will look like the figure above.

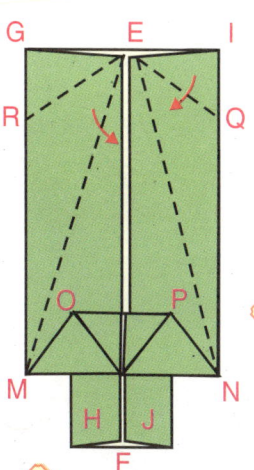

6. Tuck in point O so that it overlaps on F and makes another triangle.
Fold along ER and EQ, bringing point G and I forward. Now fold along the dotted lines.

7. Fold along EN, bringing point Q forward.

8. Turn the paper over and decorate with sketch pen.

Duck

HEAD

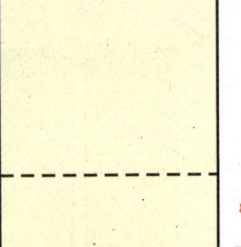

1. Take a rectangular sheet. Fold into half.

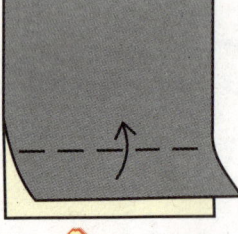

2. Fold the upper side of the sheet.

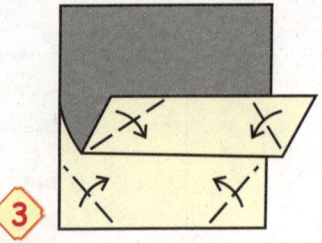

3. Fold the corners in the direction of the arrows.

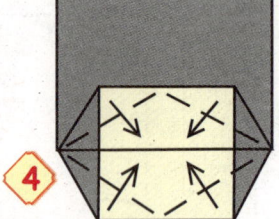

4. Fold the corners inwards in the direction of the arrows.

5. Fold the top corners backwards in the direction of arrows.

6. Stick round pieces of white paper and draw the eyeballs with a black pen.

BODY

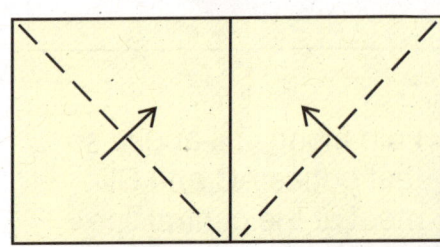

1. Fold both the corners inside of another rectangular paper.

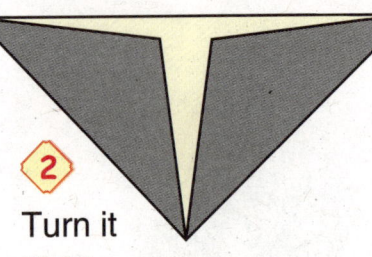

2. Turn it over.

3. Fold inwards in the direction of the arrows.

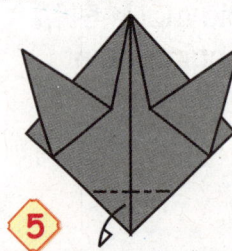

4. Fold the corners upward in the direction of the arrows.

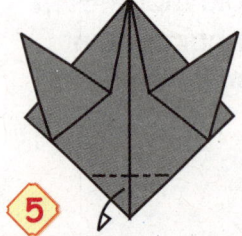

5. Fold the lower tip backwards along the dotted line.

6. Your figure will look like the one given above.

7. Now stick the head on the top of the body.

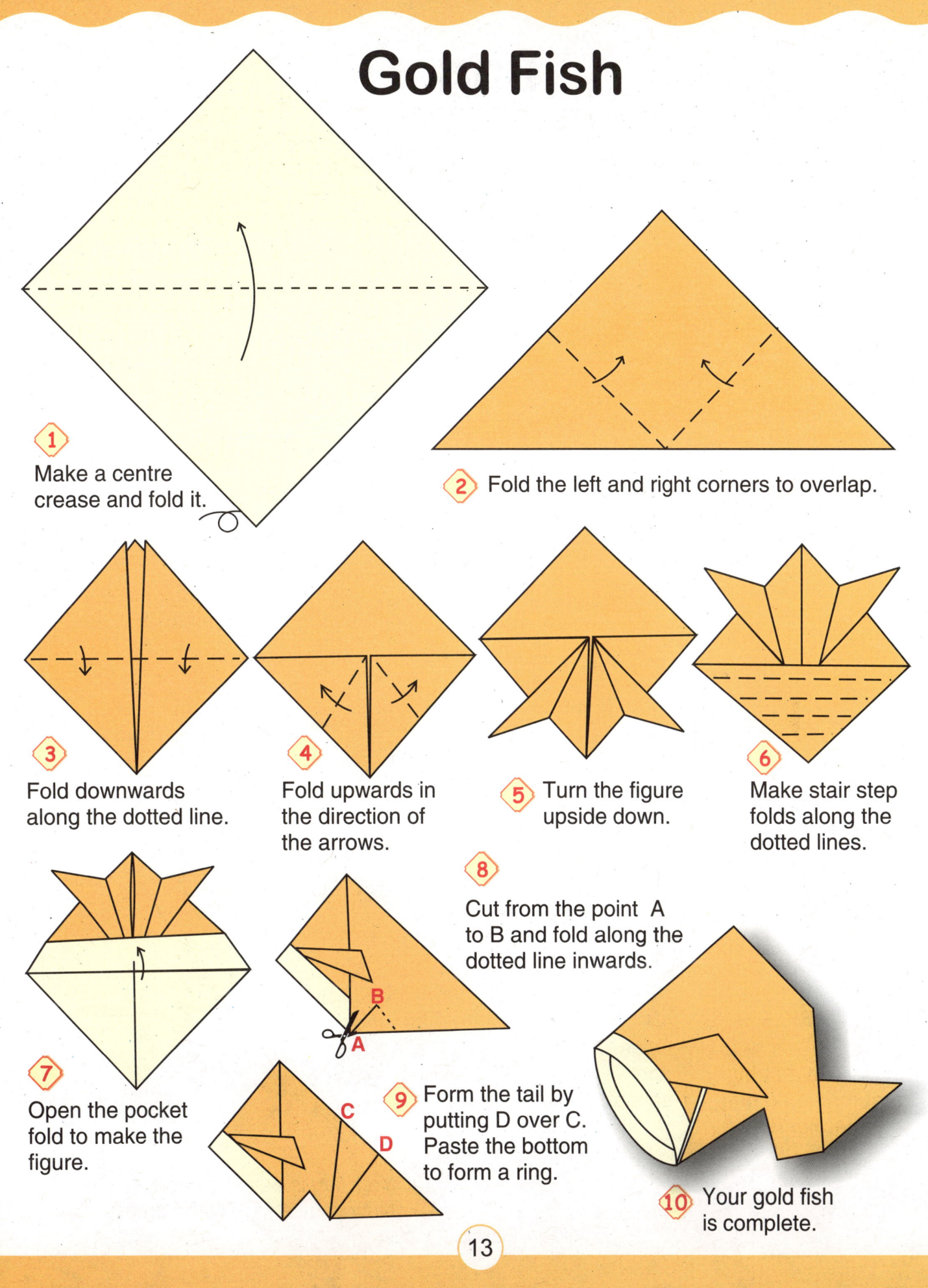

Fan

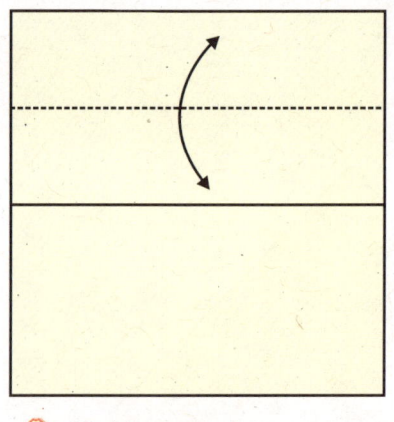

① Fold to make creases and fold back.

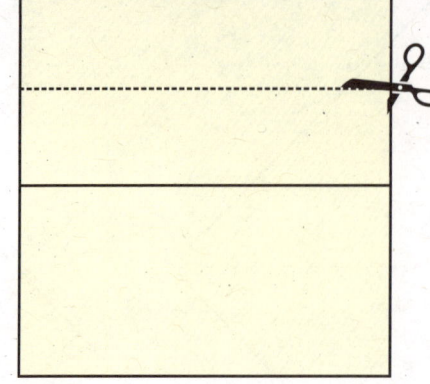

② Cut with a pair of scissors.

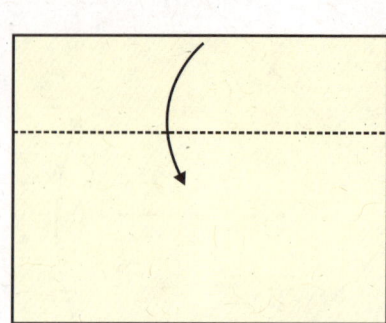

③ Fold along the dotted line.

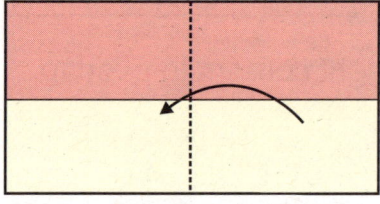

④ Fold along the dotted line and unfold.

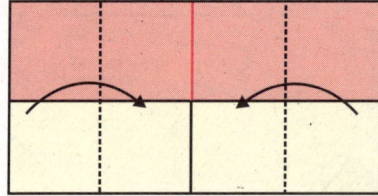

⑤ Fold to meet the centre line.

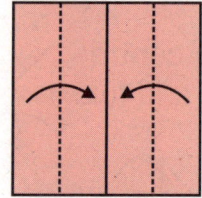

⑥ Fold to meet the centre line.

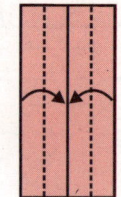

⑦ Fold again to meet the centre line.

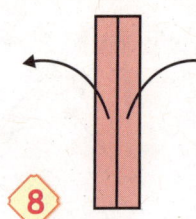

⑧ Now unfold.

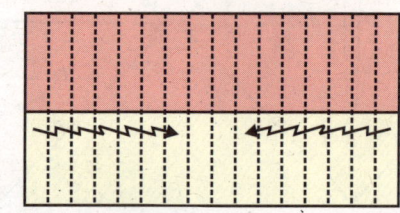

⑨ Step fold along the dotted lines.

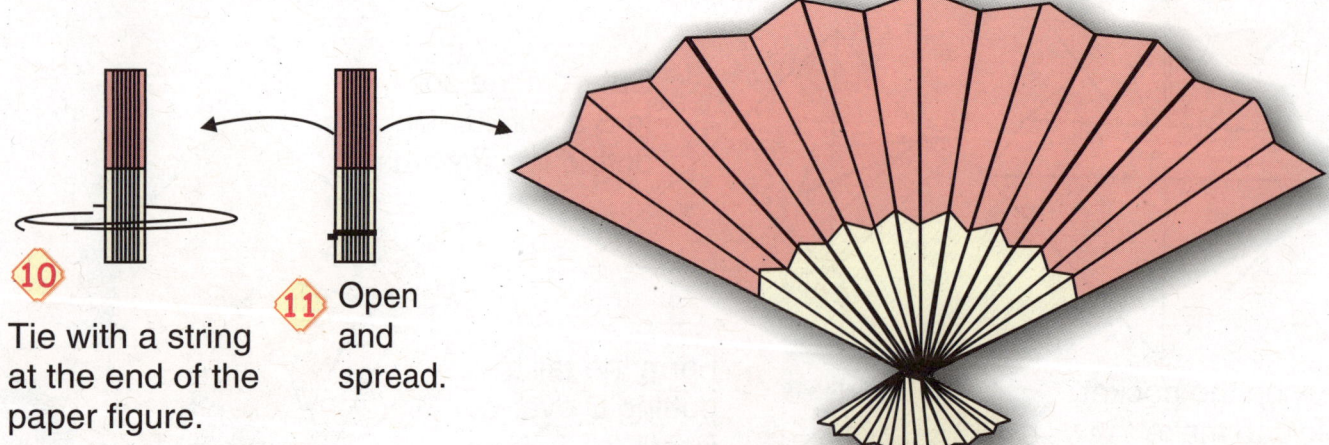

⑩ Tie with a string at the end of the paper figure.

⑪ Open and spread.

⑫ Your fan is at last complete. Now you can enjoy the breeze.

Wind Mill

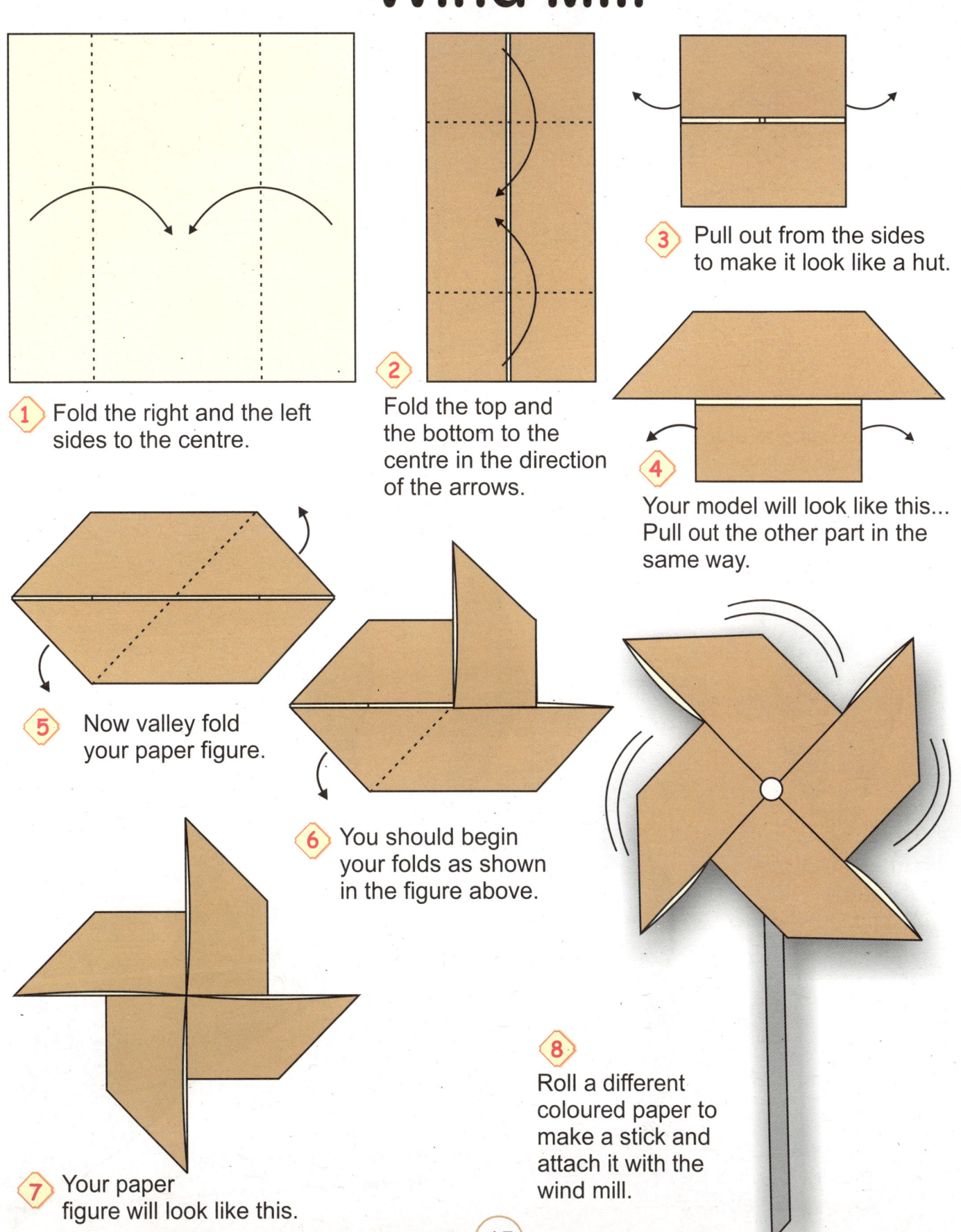

1. Fold the right and the left sides to the centre.
2. Fold the top and the bottom to the centre in the direction of the arrows.
3. Pull out from the sides to make it look like a hut.
4. Your model will look like this... Pull out the other part in the same way.
5. Now valley fold your paper figure.
6. You should begin your folds as shown in the figure above.
7. Your paper figure will look like this.
8. Roll a different coloured paper to make a stick and attach it with the wind mill.

15

Leaf

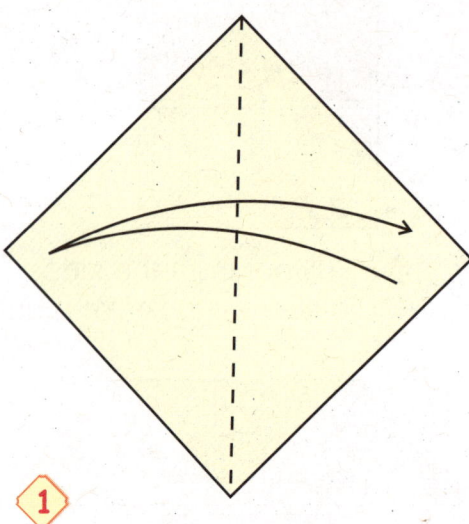

1. Fold into half and unfold to get a centre line.

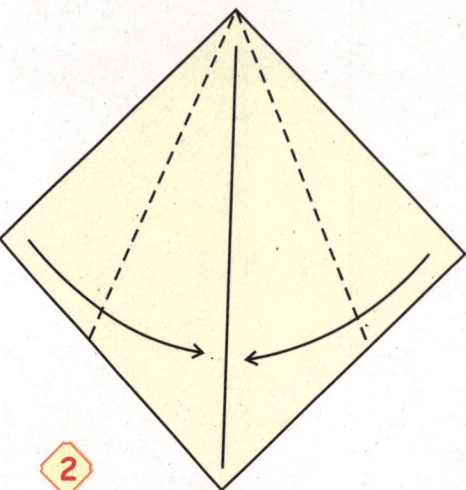

2. Fold the right and left corners to the centre line.

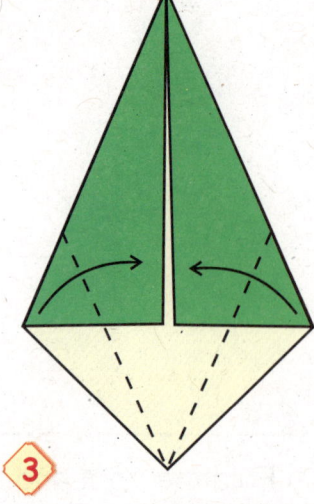

3. Again fold the corners as shown here.

4. Fold backwards into half.

5. Make slanting folds forwards and backwards alternately.

6. Your paper figure should look like the one shown above.

7. Now open your paper figure. Your green leaf is complete.

Shoe

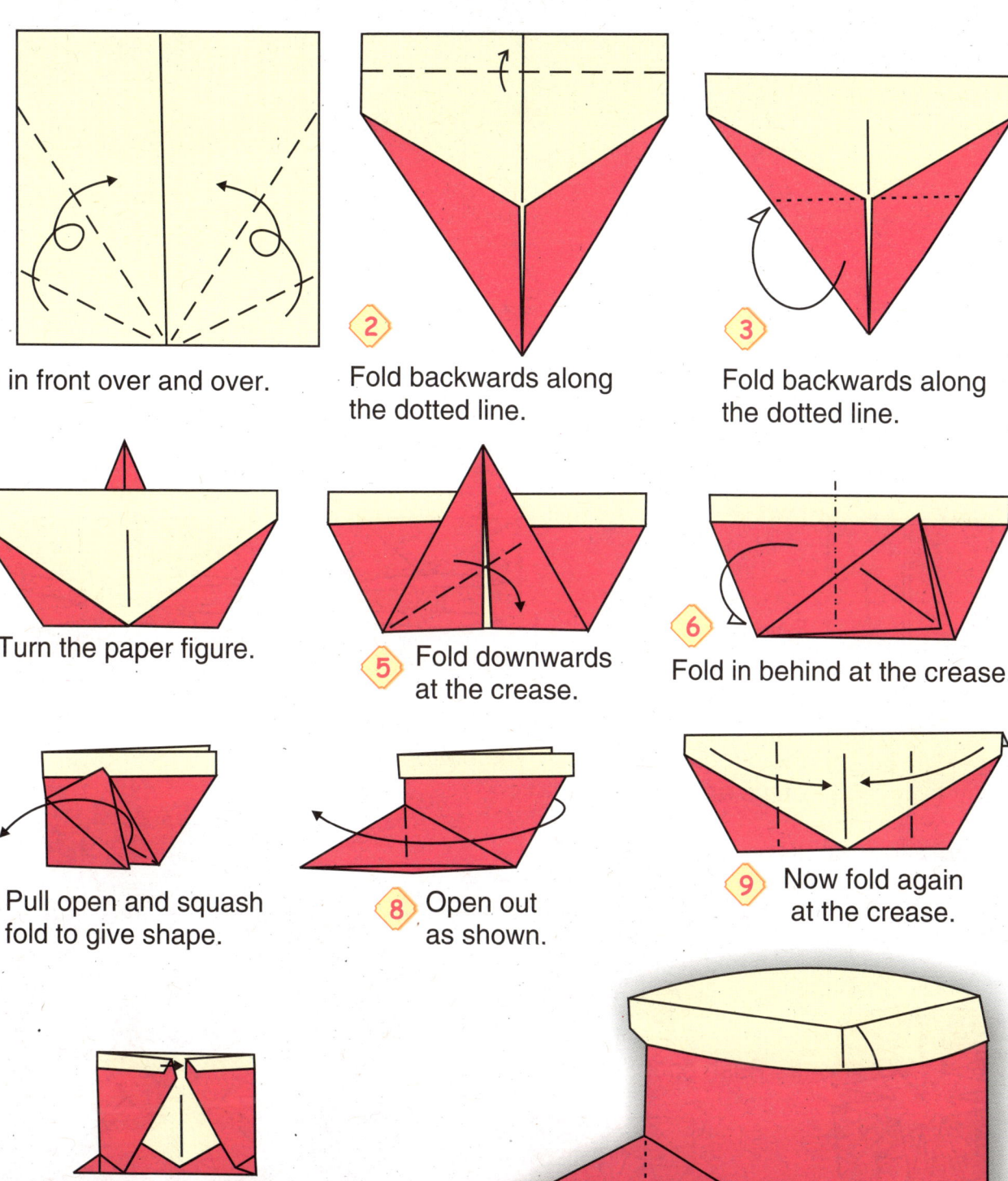

1. Fold in front over and over.
2. Fold backwards along the dotted line.
3. Fold backwards along the dotted line.
4. Turn the paper figure.
5. Fold downwards at the crease.
6. Fold in behind at the crease.
7. Pull open and squash fold to give shape.
8. Open out as shown.
9. Now fold again at the crease.
10. Insert the top corners into one another to interlock.
11. Bingo! Your shoe is ready to be worn.

Badge

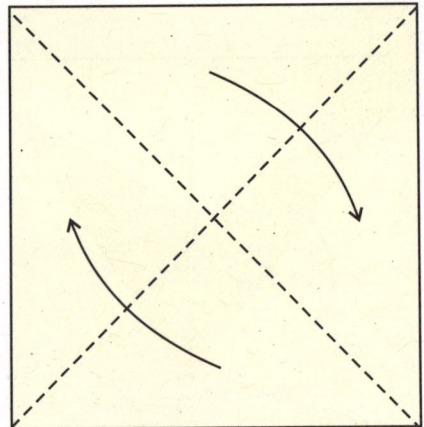

1. Join the opposite corners to make creases.

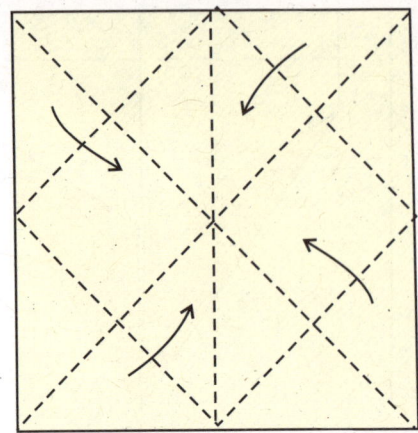

2. Fold the corners inwards and reopen.

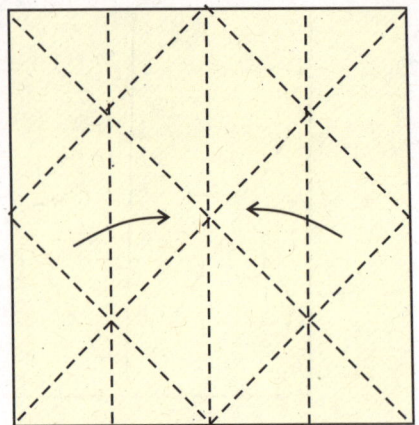

3. Make three folds as shown.

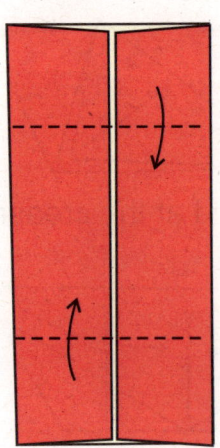

4. Fold the top and the bottom parts along the dotted lines in the direction of the arrows.

5. Open the top and the bottom edges.

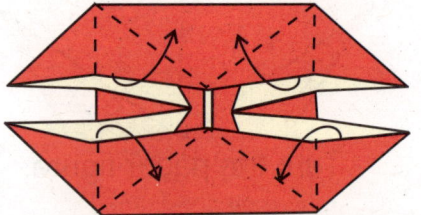

6. Open the pockets as shown.

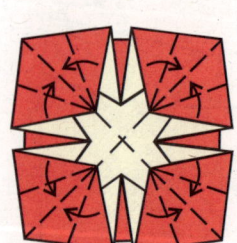

7. Fold along the dotted lines in the direction of the arrows.

8. Push open the little pockets.

9. Fold four corners backwards.

10. Paste a round piece of paper in the centre of the badge. Your badge is ready to wear.

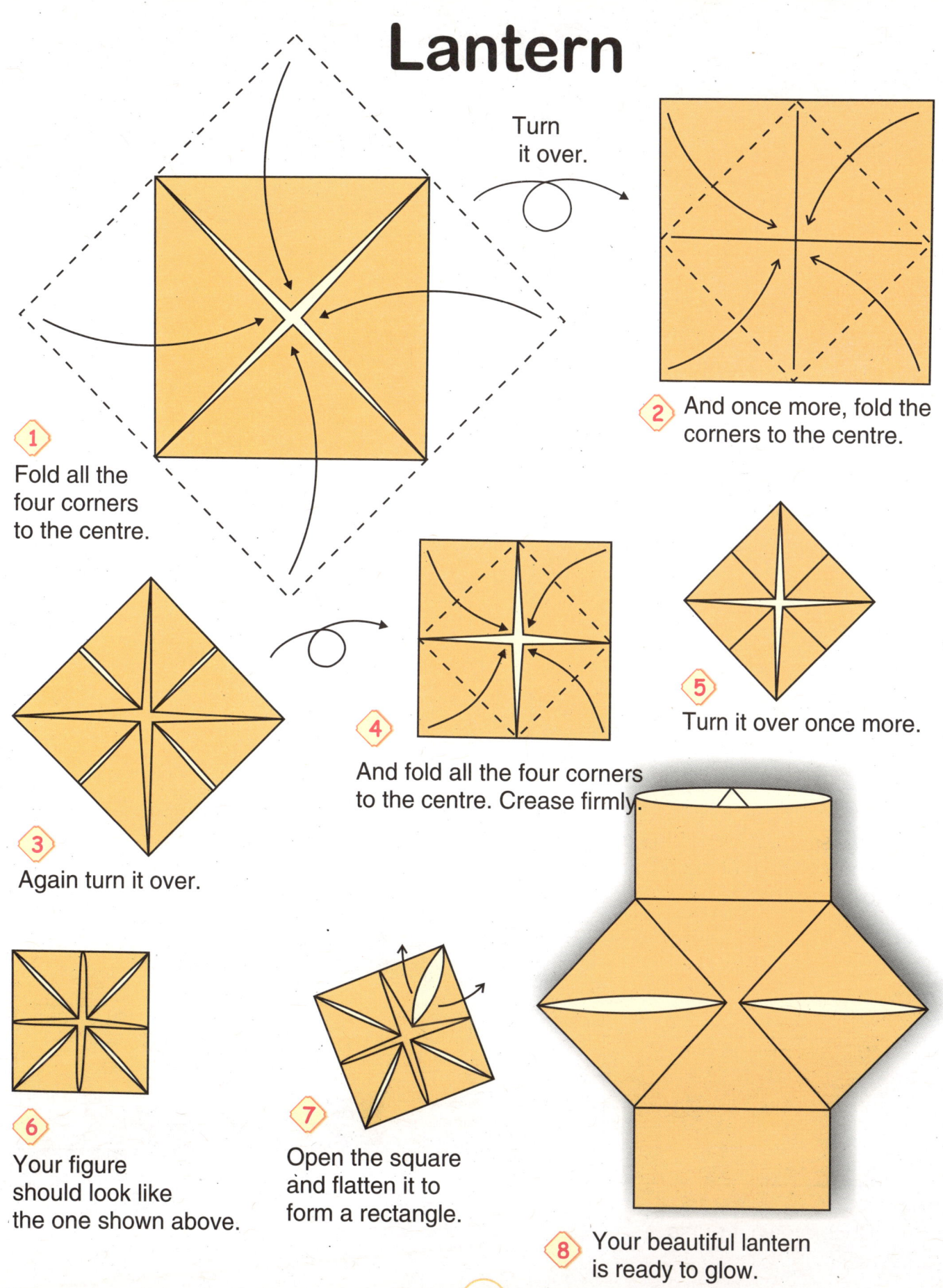

Purse

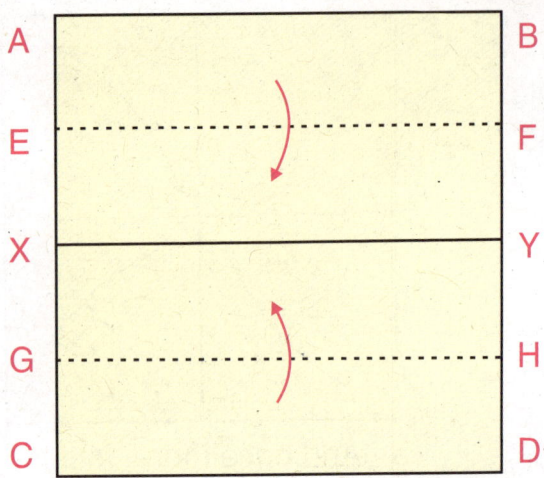

② Turn the paper figure.

① Crease it in the middle along XY. Then fold along EF so that AB falls on XY. Similarly fold along GH.

④ Turn the paper figure. Now fold the paper figure in the direction of the arrows.

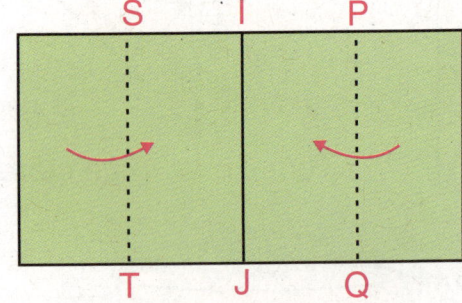

③ Crease the paper in the middle along IJ. Fold along ST and PQ towards IJ.

⑥ Your purse is ready to be used.

⑤ Decorate your purse.

20

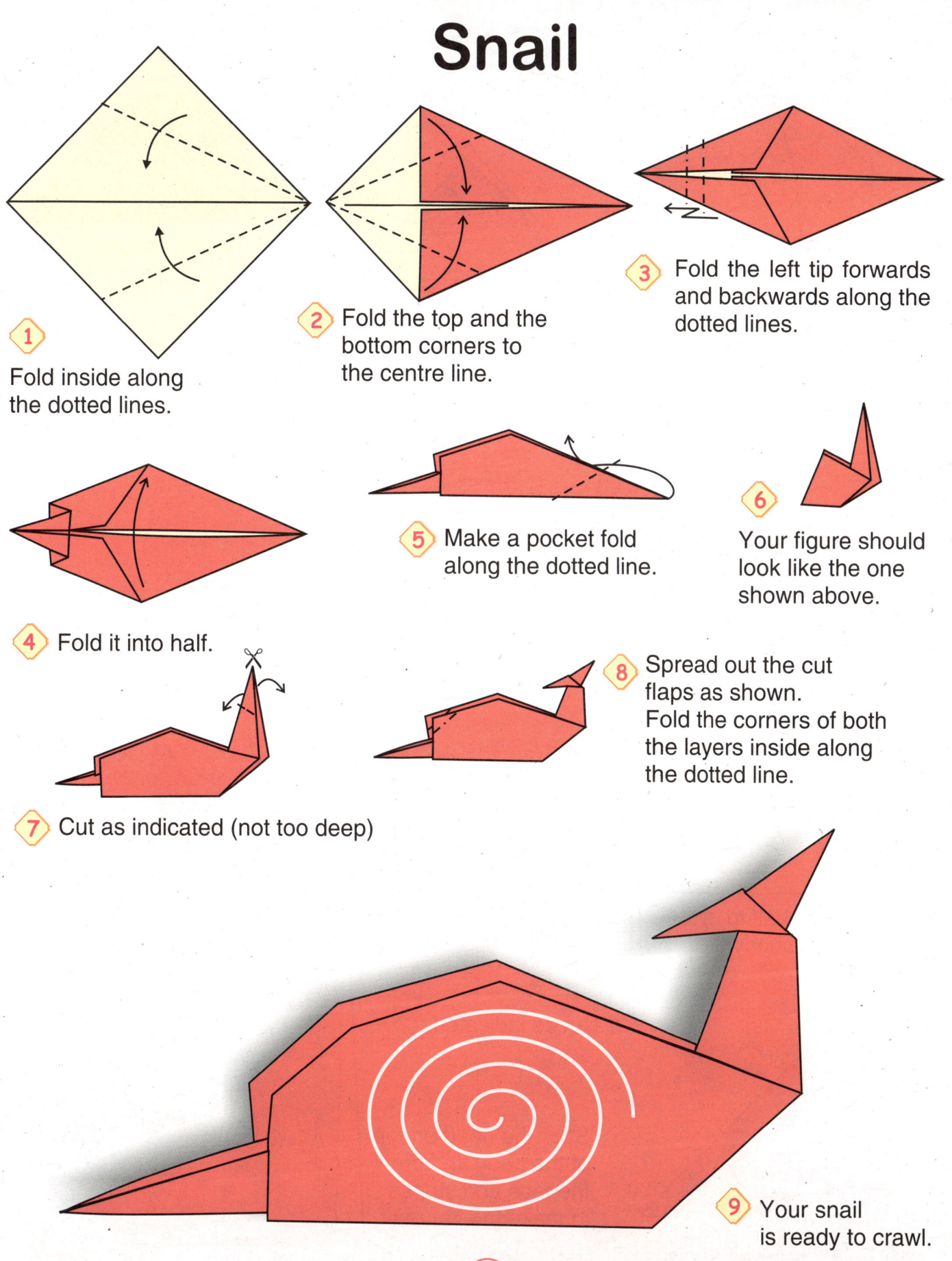

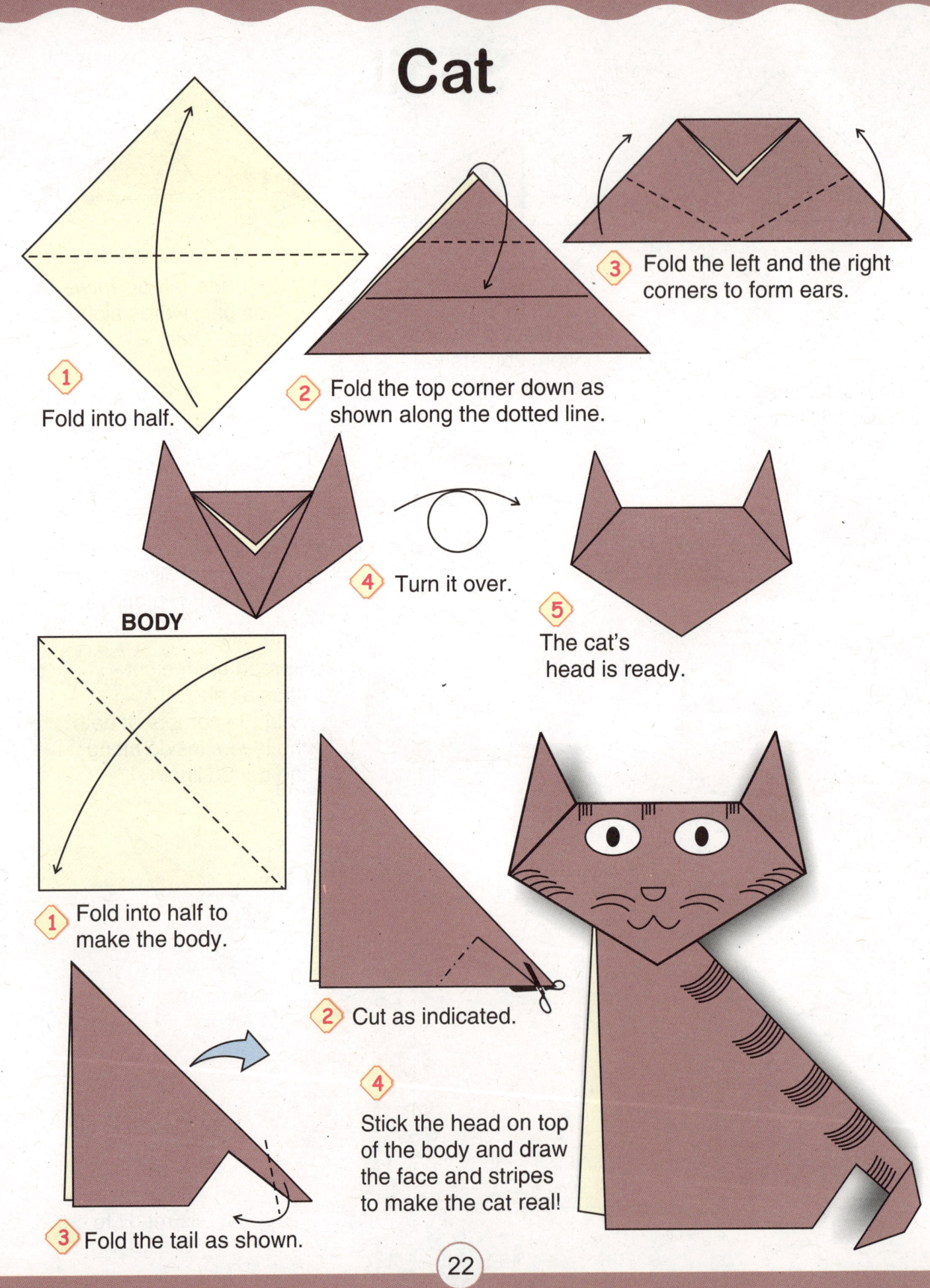

Pendulum Clock

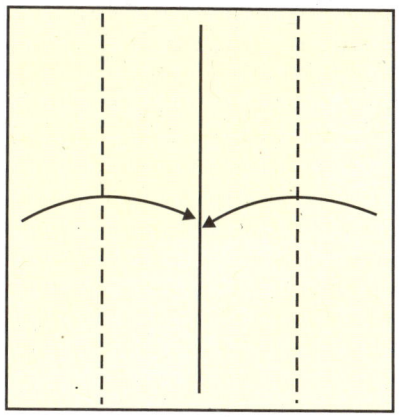

◆ 1
Find the centre line of the paper and fold the left and the right edges to it.

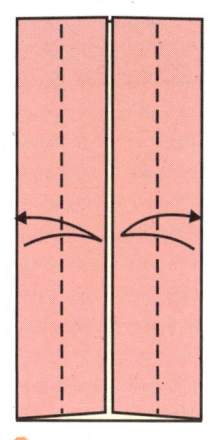

◆ 2
Fold similarly once more and unfold.

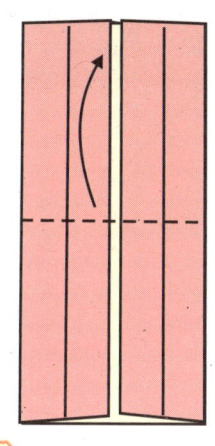

◆ 3
Fold into half from top to bottom and unfold.

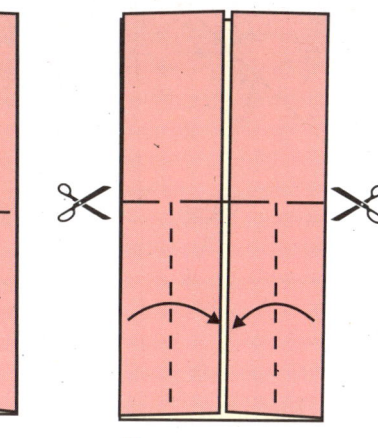

◆ 4
Cut as shown and fold both the lower flaps along the dotted lines.

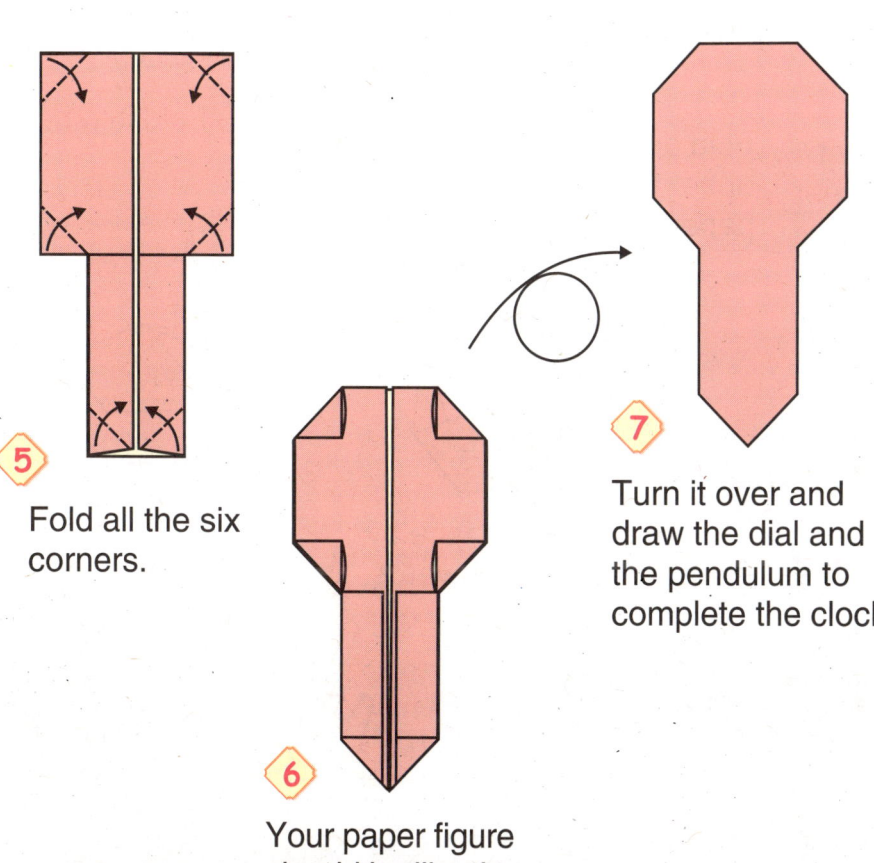

◆ 5
Fold all the six corners.

◆ 6
Your paper figure should be like the one above.

◆ 7
Turn it over and draw the dial and the pendulum to complete the clock.

◆ 8
Voila! Your clock is ready to tick.

Cock

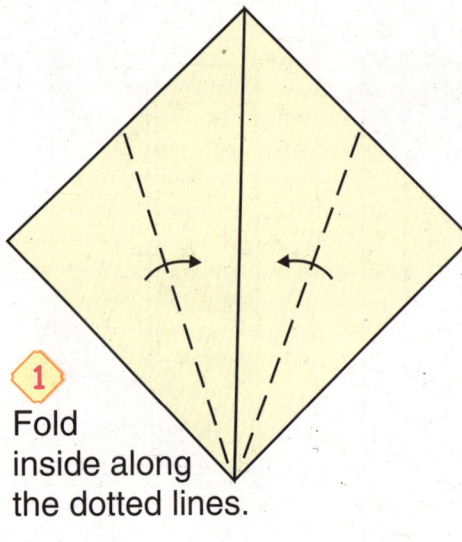

① Fold inside along the dotted lines.

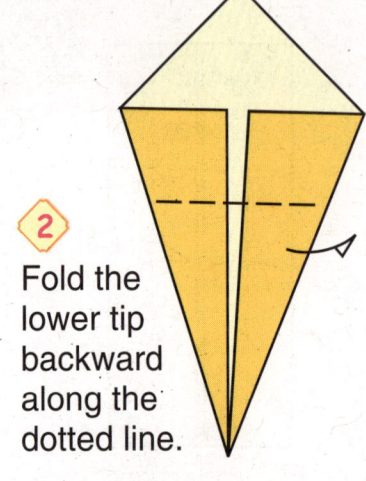

② Fold the lower tip backward along the dotted line.

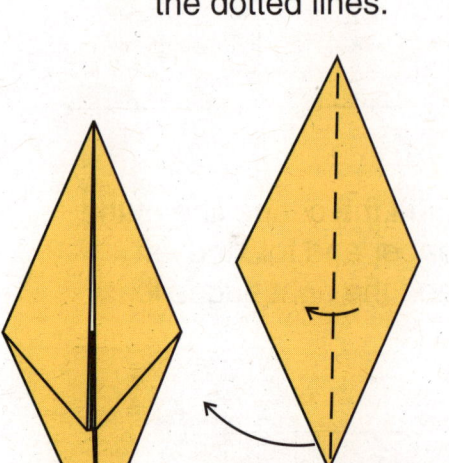

③ Fold inside along the dotted lines.

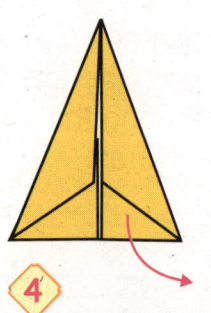

④ Make a pocket fold in the direction of arrow.

⑤ Make a pocket fold on the other side in the same way.

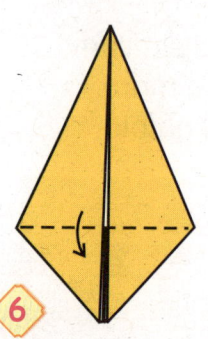

⑥ Fold down the upper tip of the paper figure.

⑦ Turn over.

⑧ Fold into half.

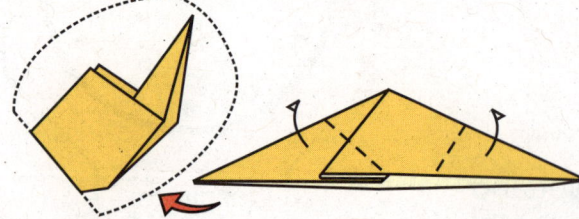

⑨ Fold it inwards along the dotted lines.

⑩ Make the face by folding it inwards.

⑪ Fold it inwards along the dotted lines to bring out the legs.

⑫ Fold again inwards along the dotted lines.

⑬ Make cuts in the tail.

⑭ Attach a cockscomb by cutting it out from a separate piece of red paper.

Pendulum Clock

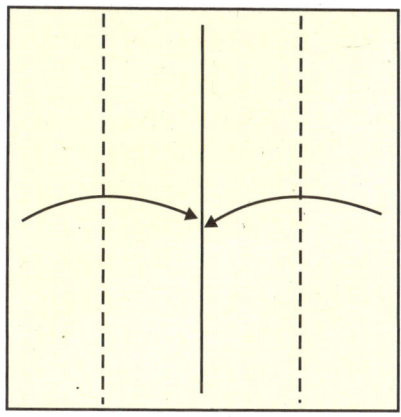

1. Find the centre line of the paper and fold the left and the right edges to it.

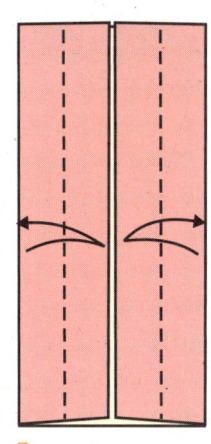

2. Fold similarly once more and unfold.

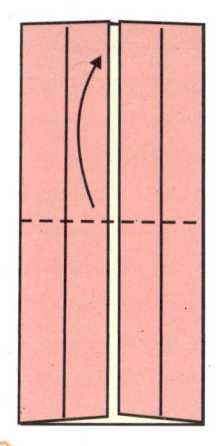

3. Fold into half from top to bottom and unfold.

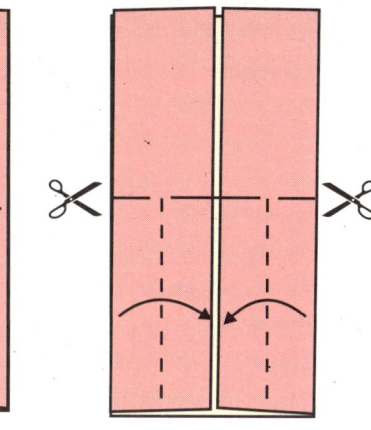

4. Cut as shown and fold both the lower flaps along the dotted lines.

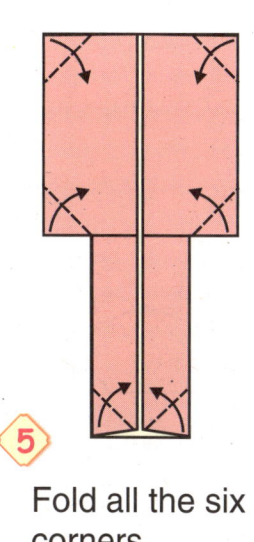

5. Fold all the six corners.

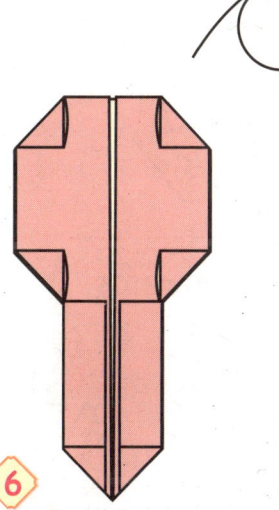

6. Your paper figure should be like the one above.

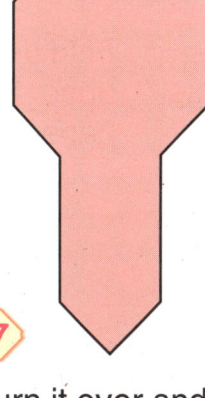

7. Turn it over and draw the dial and the pendulum to complete the clock.

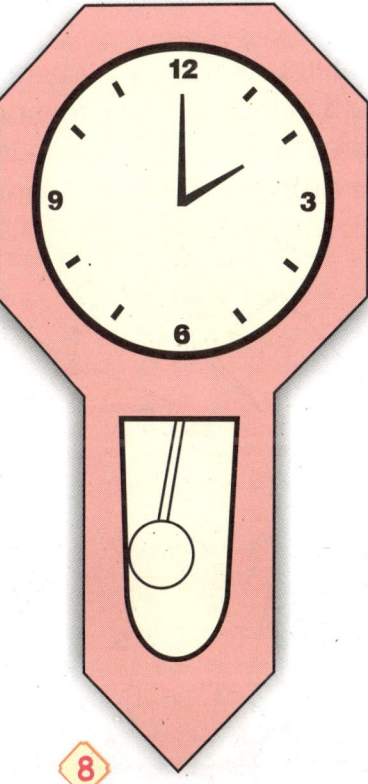

8. Voila! Your clock is ready to tick.

Cock

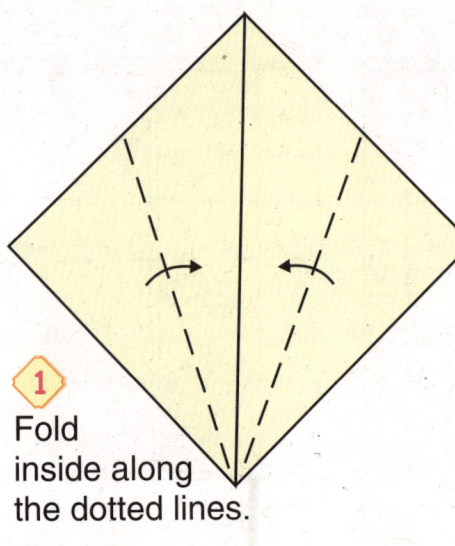

1 Fold inside along the dotted lines.

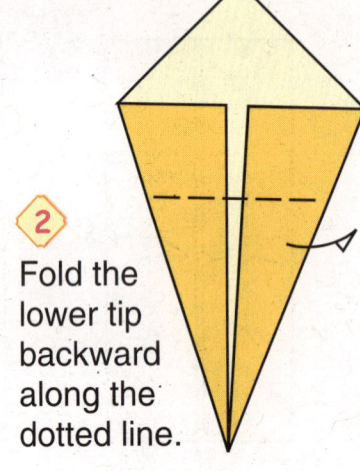

2 Fold the lower tip backward along the dotted line.

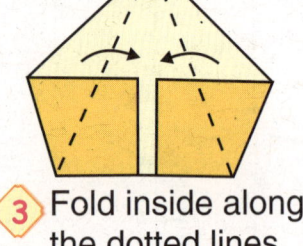

3 Fold inside along the dotted lines.

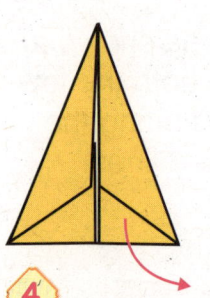

4 Make a pocket fold in the direction of arrow.

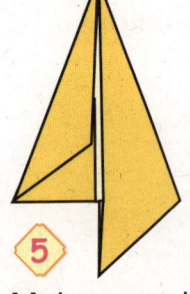

5 Make a pocket fold on the other side in the same way.

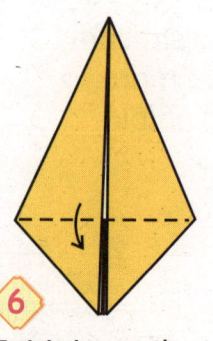

6 Fold down the upper tip of the paper figure.

7 Turn over.

8 Fold into half.

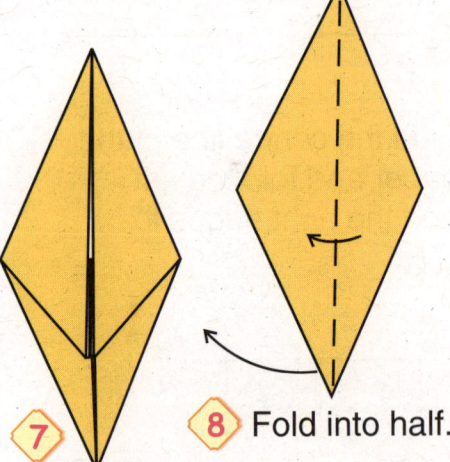

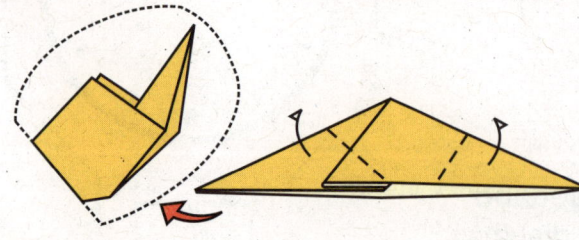

9 Fold it inwards along the dotted lines.

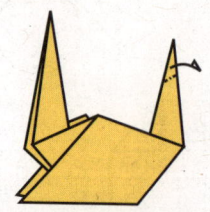

10 Make the face by folding it inwards.

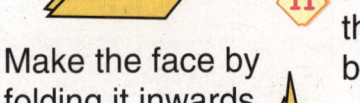

11 Fold it inwards along the dotted lines to bring out the legs.

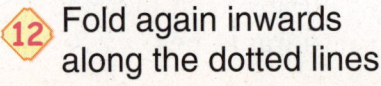

12 Fold again inwards along the dotted lines.

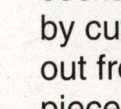

13 Make cuts in the tail.

14 Attach a cockscomb by cutting it out from a separate piece of red paper.

24